the

BRITAIN:THE FACTS

Population

Christopher Riches

FRANKLIN WATTS
LONDON•SYDNEY

First published in 2008
by Franklin Watts

Copyright © 2008 Christopher Riches and Trevor Bounford

Design by bounford.com

Franklin Watts
338 Euston Road
London NW1 3BH

Franklin Watts Australia
Level 17/207 Kent Street
Sydney, NSW 2000

All words in **bold** can be found in Glossary on pages 30–31. Website information is correct at time of going to press. However, the publishers cannot accept liability for any information or links found on third-party websites.

ISBN 978 0 7496 8383 2

Dewey classification: 304.6'0941

Printed in China

Franklin Watts is a division of Hachette Children's Books, an Hachette Livre UK company.
www.hachettelivre.co.uk

Picture credits
The publishers would like to thank the following organisations for their kind permission to reproduce illustrations in this book:

Cover image © Andrew Holt/Getty Images.
p. 8 © 2008 Esprit Photography/fotoLibra; p. 18 © Tim Graham/Getty Images; p. 22 © Ann Ronan/TopFoto; p. 23 ©2003 TopFoto; p. 24 ©1999 TopFoto.

All maps, charts and diagrams © boundford.com.

Contents

How Do We Measure Population?

Governments have always wanted to know how many people there are in their countries. This requires carrying out what is called a **census**. A census records all the people living in a country on a particular day.

The first British census?

The first census was made in Scotland – the *Senchus fer n'Alba*, made in the 7th century. It recorded men who paid tax and who were available for navy service. More famous is the Domesday Book, of 1086. It recorded all property in England. It was compiled because William I wanted more details about the country he had conquered in 1066. He used the information to raise tax.

Early censuses

The Egyptians used census information to help them plan the building of the Pyramids. They needed to know how many people could work on their construction. According to the Bible, Jesus was born in Bethlehem because Joseph and Mary had to travel there to register with the Roman authorities in a census that took place across the Roman Empire around 0 CE.

FACTS

- Before the 1801 census, people were afraid that Britain would run out of food, because no-one knew how many people lived here.
- The first full census of Britain was made in 1801.
- A census has been taken every 10 years since then.
- Computers were first used in 1961.
- The forms from the 2001 census occupy 64.5 km of shelving.
- The next census is in 2011.

H1
29 April
count me in
Census2001
England Household Fo

Why do we need a census?

A census does more than just count people. It provides information on:

- 👫 The size of families.
- 👫 How many people live in particular areas.
- 👫 How many young and old people there are.
- 👫 Where people work.
- 👫 What kind of work people do.
- 👫 What size of house people live in.

How is a census done?

A census form is delivered to every home in Britain. The form has lots of questions that must be completed. When all the questions have been answered, the form is sent to the Census office or collected by hand. All the information is then scanned into a computer and the data analysed. It now takes around a year to process all the data and produce results.

2001 census answers

The total population of Britain was 58,789,194

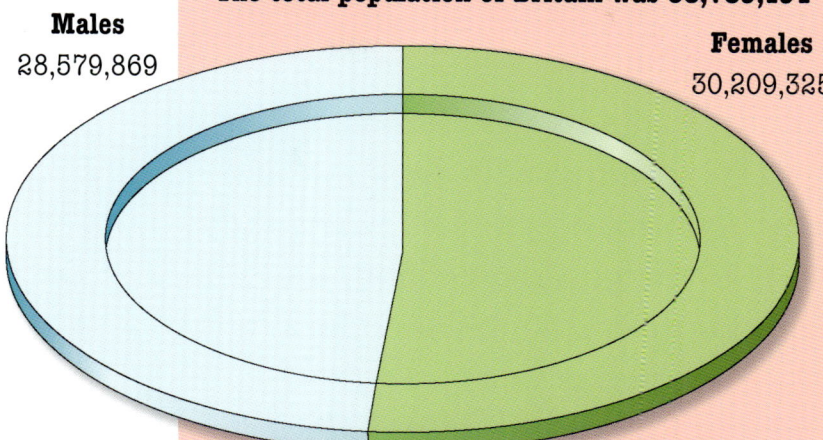

Males
28,579,869

Females
30,209,325

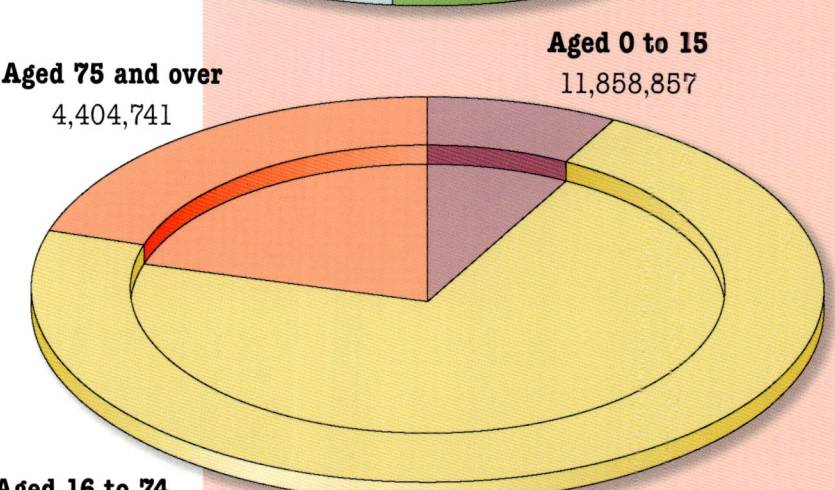

Aged 75 and over
4,404,741

Aged 0 to 15
11,858,857

Aged 16 to 74
42,525,596

All this information helps the government plan, for example:

- 👫 Where and when new schools or new hospitals are required.
- 👫 How many carers for the elderly are needed.

In between the national censuses, the Office for National Statistics makes estimates of population changes. In the pages that follow we use figures from the 2001 census and from more recent estimates from the Office for National Statistics.

How Many People Live Here?

It is important to know how many people live in Britain. If we know how many people live here, and where they live, then the government and businesses can plan for the future. The population of Britain (England, Scotland, Wales and Northern Ireland) in 2006 was 60.6 million.

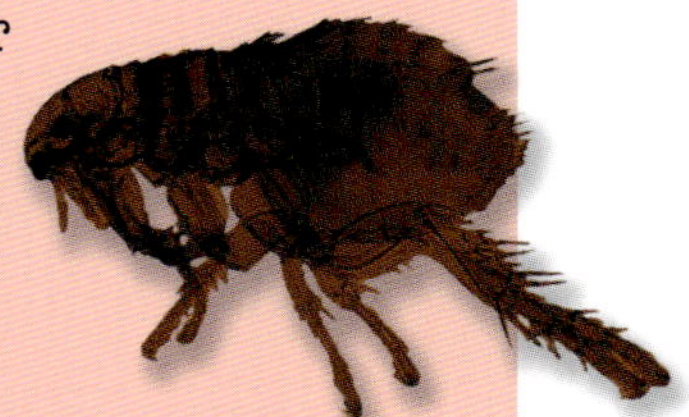

How has the population grown?

The diagram shows the growth of the population in England. Before 1801 (when the first official count was made), the figures are estimates. This graph just shows England because similar figures for the rest of Britain are not known. Note the fall in population between 1300 and 1400 and the very fast growth between 1801 and 1901.

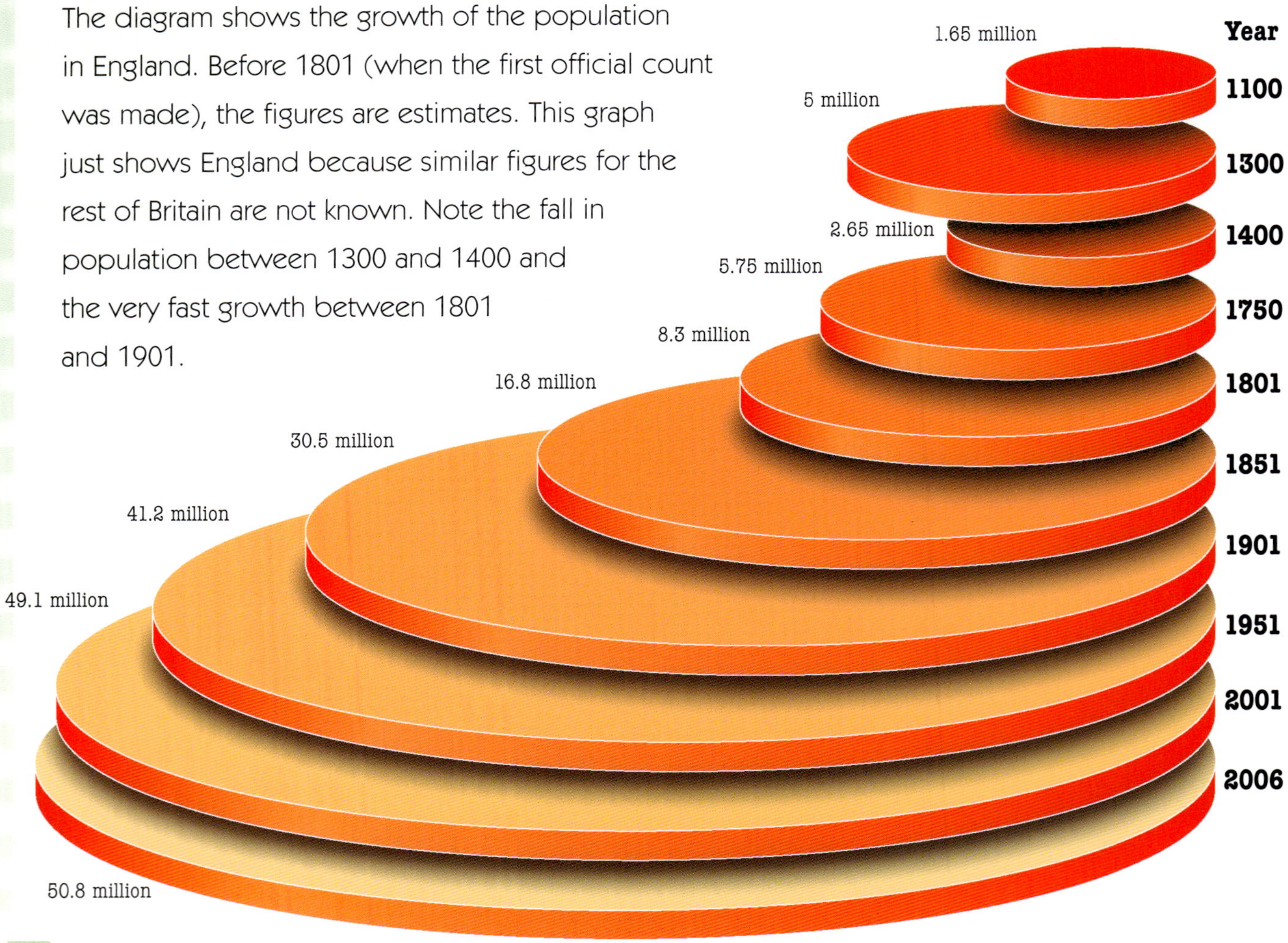

The Black Death

The population of England almost halved between 1300 and 1400. What caused such a change?

- Famine. There was not enough food for everyone because of poor harvests.
- Disease. Over a third of the population was killed between 1348 and 1350 by the Black Death, a very **infectious** disease. This is a disease passed from fleas to humans.

	Year
1.65 million	1100
5 million	1300
2.65 million	1400
5.75 million	1750
8.3 million	1801
16.8 million	1851
30.5 million	1901
41.2 million	1951
49.1 million	2001
50.8 million	2006

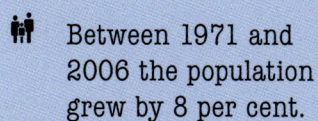

- Between 1971 and 2006 the population grew by 8 per cent.
- Since 2001, the population has been growing at 0.5 per cent a year. This is a much slower rate than in the previous 10 years.
- In 2006 45 per cent of the population growth was caused by there being more births than deaths. People coming to Britain from overseas made up 55 per cent.

And how will the population grow?

Experts try to **predict** how the population will grow. Here is what they think might happen.

The total population will rise from 60.6 million in 2006 to 69.4 million in 2026, a growth of 14.5%.

Industrialisation

Between 1801 and 1901 the population increased by five times. What caused this very fast growth?

- **Agricultural** improvements, so there was more food and less risk of famine.
- Improved medical knowledge and diets, so people lived longer.
- Development of industry, requiring more workers and creating wealth.

These changes led to the rapid growth of towns: Birmingham grew from a small town to a major city.

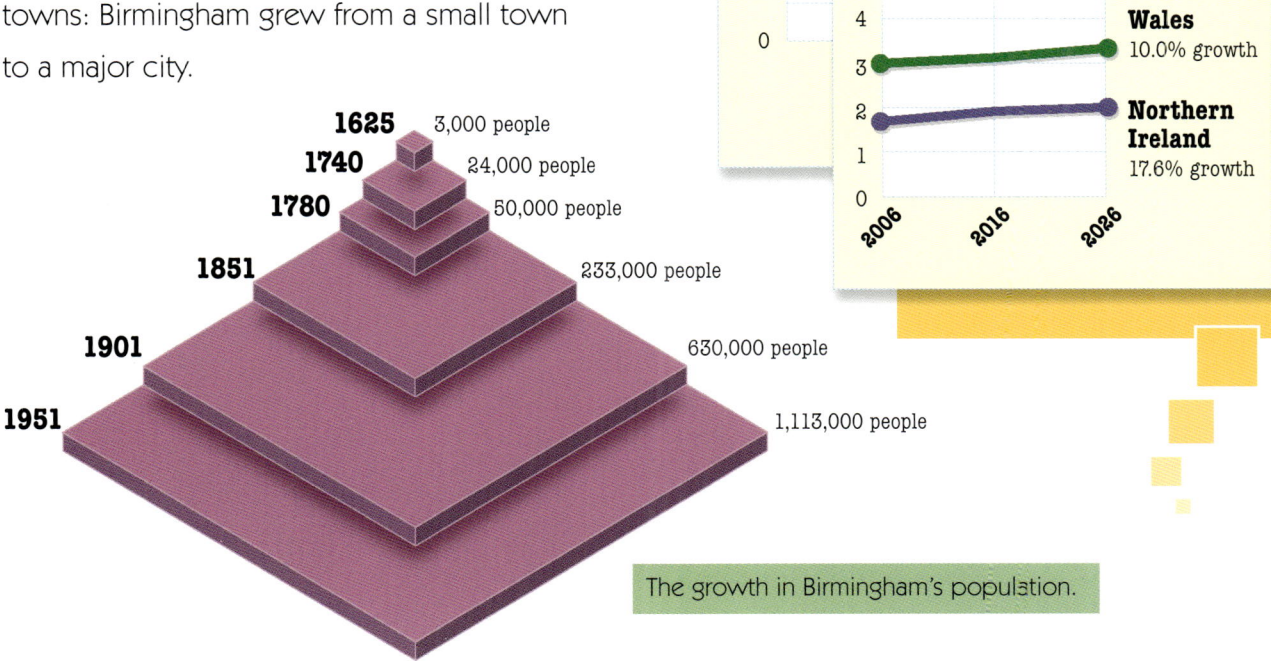

Year	Population
1625	3,000 people
1740	24,000 people
1780	50,000 people
1851	233,000 people
1901	630,000 people
1951	1,113,000 people

England 15.6% growth
Scotland 6.0% growth
Wales 10.0% growth
Northern Ireland 17.6% growth

The growth in Birmingham's population.

Why Does the Population Change?

The population of Britain has changed a lot over the years. An increasing population can be caused by:

● more births than deaths,
● people living longer,
● more people coming into the country than leaving it.

Number of births

The number of babies born each year is a key measure of how the population is growing. In the last 100 years in Britain there has been a big decline in the number of babies born. For every 1,000 women aged 15 to 44, there were about 110 births in 1905, but by 2006 this had fallen to 60. The number of births fell from just over 1 million in 1901 to just under 750,000 in 2006. This figure was even smaller in 2001 but it has been rising since then.

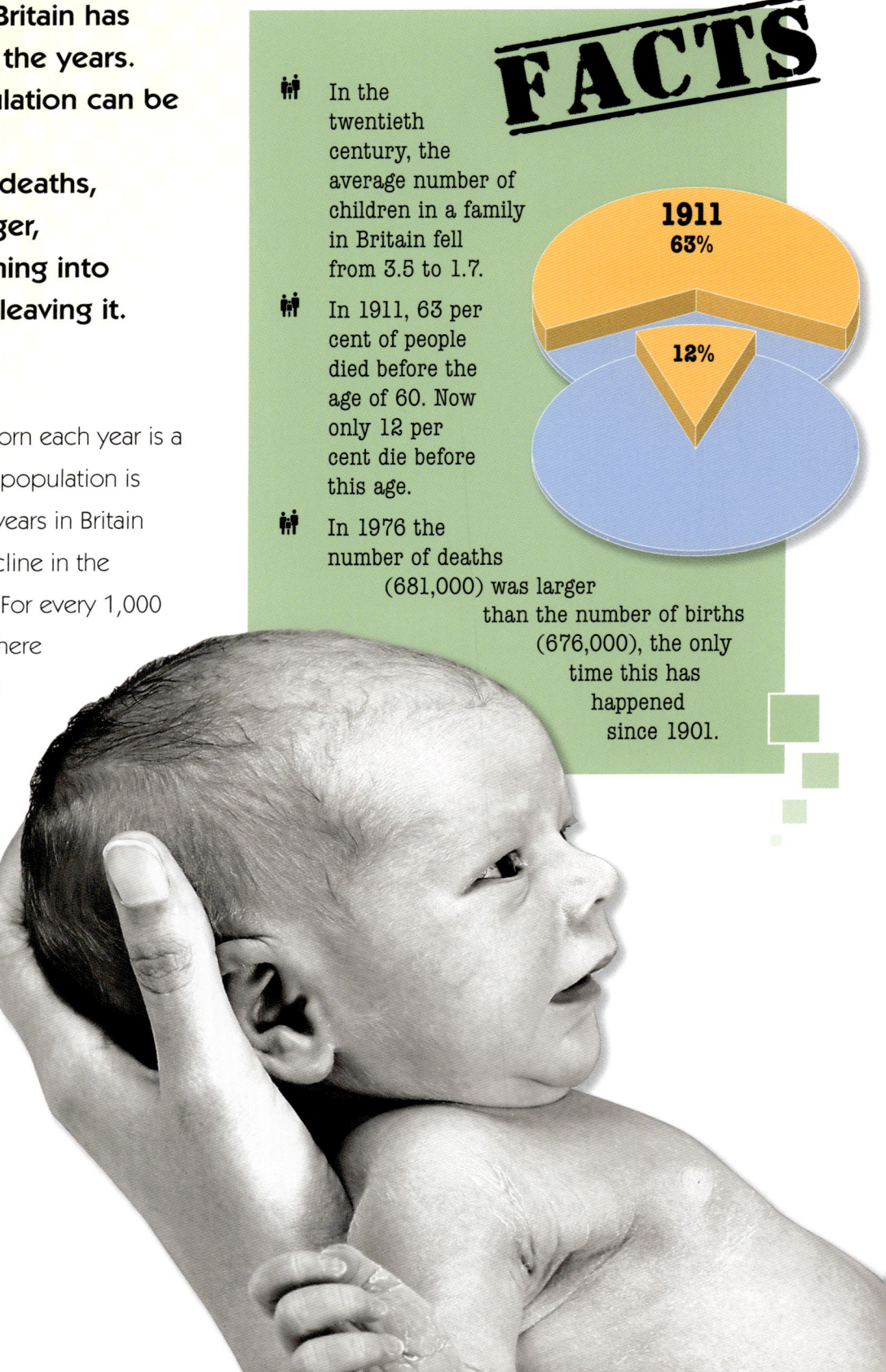

FACTS

● In the twentieth century, the average number of children in a family in Britain fell from 3.5 to 1.7.

● In 1911, 63 per cent of people died before the age of 60. Now only 12 per cent die before this age.

● In 1976 the number of deaths (681,000) was larger than the number of births (676,000), the only time this has happened since 1901.

1911
63%

12%

Life expectancy

Life expectancy is an estimate of how long, on average, a person will live. In 1901 baby boys were expected to live for 45 years and girls 49 years. By 2005 baby boys were expected to live for 77 years and baby girls for 81 years. Glasgow has the lowest life expectancy in Britain, an average of 73 years. But this is not the whole picture. Within Glasgow, life expectancy for a boy born in the deprived Calton district is estimated at 54 years while for a boy born in Bearsden, a wealthy suburb, it is over 80 years.

Number of deaths

In 1901 there were 632,000 deaths and in 2006, 572,000. As the population has increased by over 20 million in the same period, we must be living longer.

Infant mortality

A hundred years ago many babies died when they were very young. Advances in medicine and improvements in housing and child care mean that far fewer young babies die. The chart shows what happened in England and Wales.

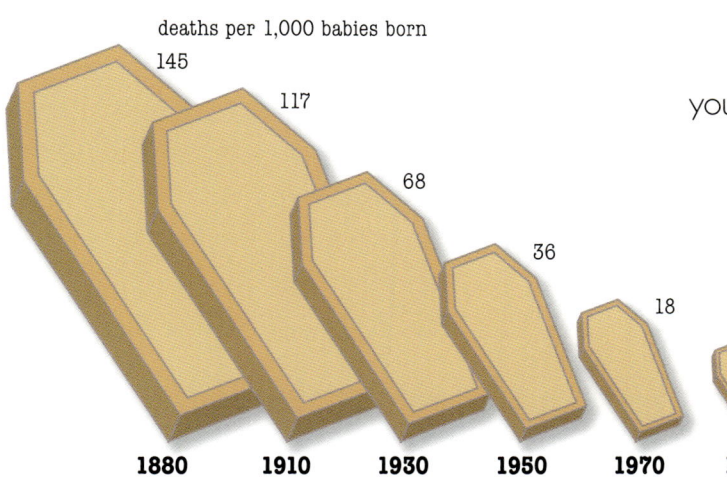

deaths per 1,000 babies born

145	117	68	36	18	9	5
1880	1910	1930	1950	1970	1990	2006

Migration

The other factor that influences population growth is the number of people who leave the country to live elsewhere in the world (**emigration**) and the number of people who come to live in Britain from overseas (**immigration**). Until fairly recently there were more people leaving than arriving. In 1981 237,000 people left and 204,000 arrived. However, in the late 1980s the position was reversed and in 2006, 400,000 people left and 591,000 arrived, giving an increase of 191,000 people.

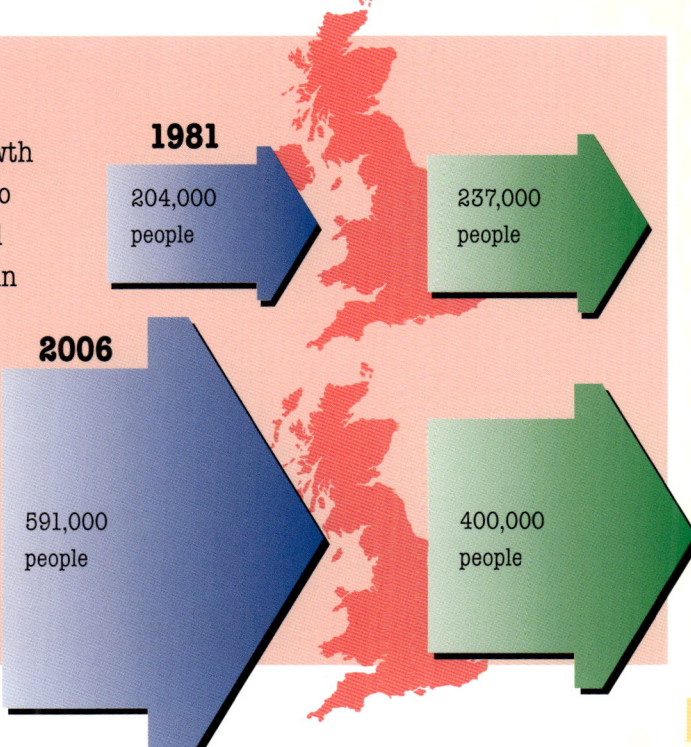

1981

204,000 people

237,000 people

2006

591,000 people

400,000 people

How is the Population Made Up?

Knowing more about the population make up will help in planning for the future. If the number of children is increasing, then more schools will be needed. If people are living longer, then it will cost more to provide pensions.

Population pyramids

These diagrams are called **population pyramids**. They show the age and sex of the population.

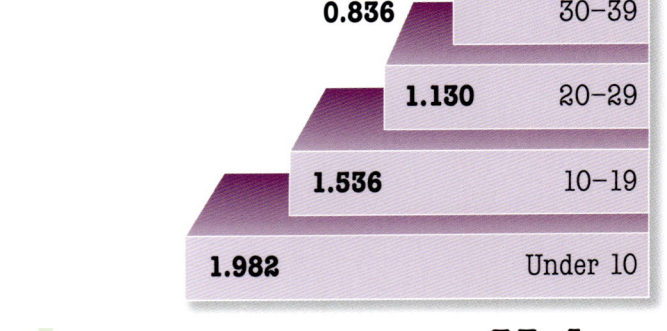

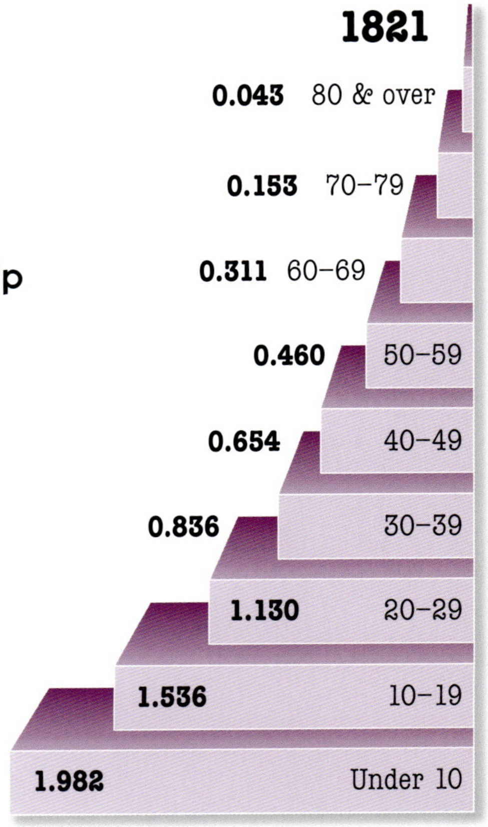

1821

0.043	80 & over
0.153	70–79
0.311	60–69
0.460	50–59
0.654	40–49
0.836	30–39
1.130	20–29
1.536	10–19
1.982	Under 10

Males
(millions)

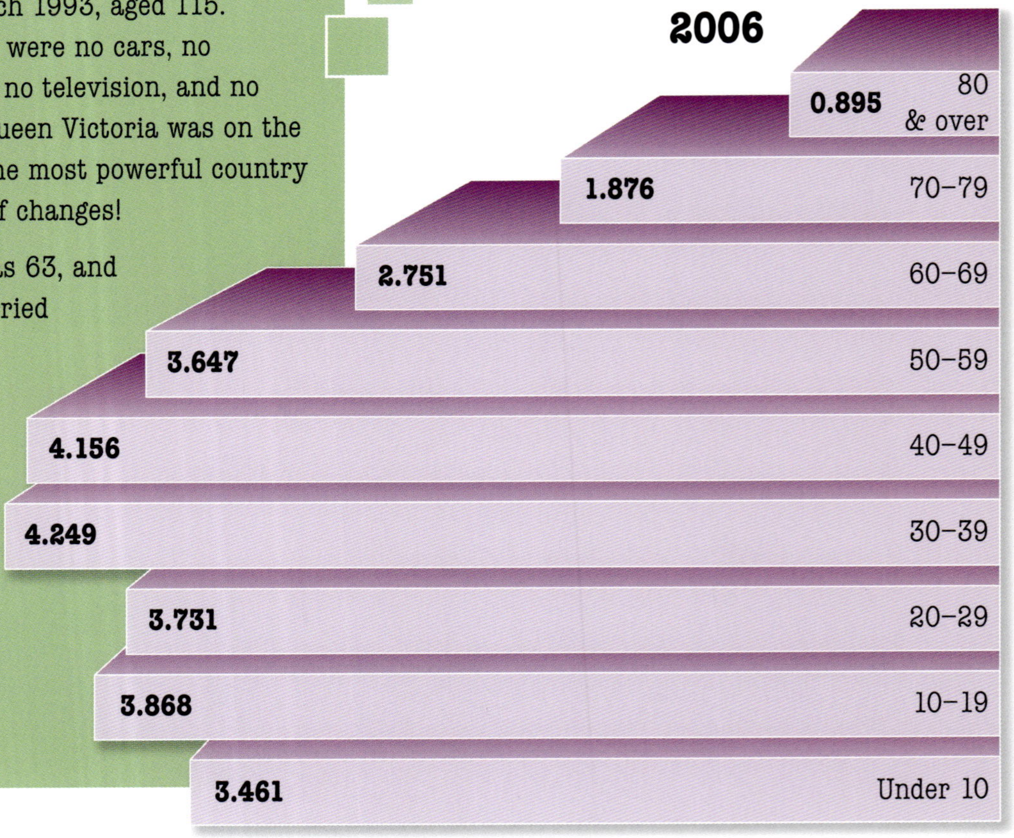

2006

0.895	80 & over
1.876	70–79
2.751	60–69
3.647	50–59
4.156	40–49
4.249	30–39
3.731	20–29
3.868	10–19
3.461	Under 10

Britain's oldest person

Charlotte Marion Hughes was born on 1 August 1877 and died on 17 March 1993, aged 115. When she was born there were no cars, no aeroplanes, no telephone, no television, and no electricity in the home. Queen Victoria was on the throne and Britain was the most powerful country in the world. What a lot of changes!

She married when she was 63, and then had 40 years of married life before her husband died. In 1987, she flew across the Atlantic on Concorde, becoming the oldest person ever to fly.

She put her long life down to 'a good honest life'.

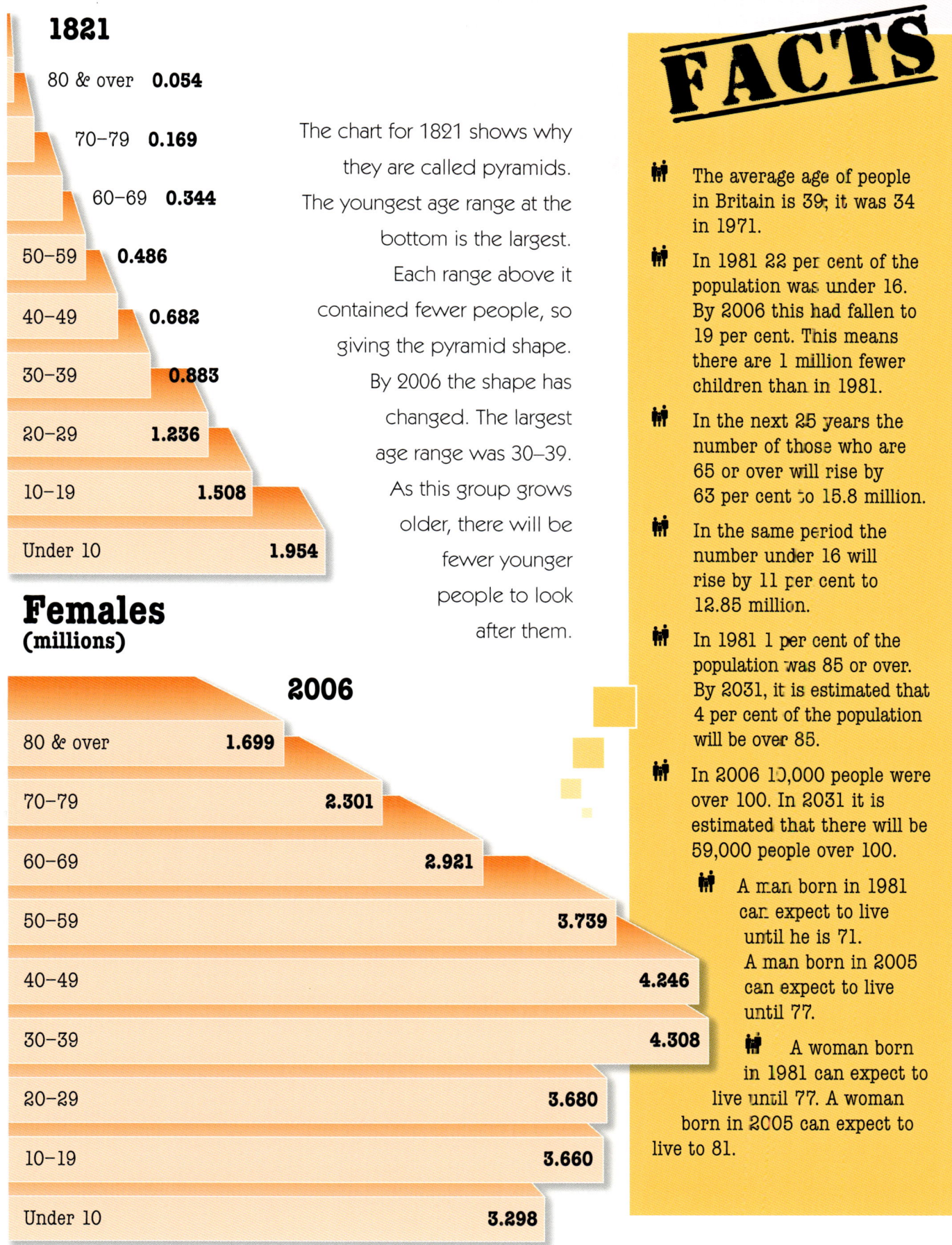

1821

80 & over	**0.054**
70–79	**0.169**
60–69	**0.344**
50–59	**0.486**
40–49	**0.682**
30–39	**0.883**
20–29	**1.236**
10–19	**1.508**
Under 10	**1.954**

Females
(millions)

The chart for 1821 shows why they are called pyramids. The youngest age range at the bottom is the largest. Each range above it contained fewer people, so giving the pyramid shape. By 2006 the shape has changed. The largest age range was 30–39. As this group grows older, there will be fewer younger people to look after them.

2006

80 & over	**1.699**
70–79	**2.301**
60–69	**2.921**
50–59	**3.739**
40–49	**4.246**
30–39	**4.308**
20–29	**3.680**
10–19	**3.660**
Under 10	**3.298**

FACTS

- The average age of people in Britain is 39; it was 34 in 1971.

- In 1981 22 per cent of the population was under 16. By 2006 this had fallen to 19 per cent. This means there are 1 million fewer children than in 1981.

- In the next 25 years the number of those who are 65 or over will rise by 63 per cent to 15.8 million.

- In the same period the number under 16 will rise by 11 per cent to 12.85 million.

- In 1981 1 per cent of the population was 85 or over. By 2031, it is estimated that 4 per cent of the population will be over 85.

- In 2006 10,000 people were over 100. In 2031 it is estimated that there will be 59,000 people over 100.

- A man born in 1981 can expect to live until he is 71. A man born in 2005 can expect to live until 77.

- A woman born in 1981 can expect to live until 77. A woman born in 2005 can expect to live to 81.

Where Do We Live?

Even when we know how many people live in Britain, it is very important to know where those people live. The **distribution** of the population is very uneven. Most people live in towns and cities. Only a few people live in isolated rural communities.

Scotland
5,100,000

Northern Ireland
1,700,000

Northern Ireland 123 People per km^2

Scotland 65 People per km^2

Wales 143 People per km^2

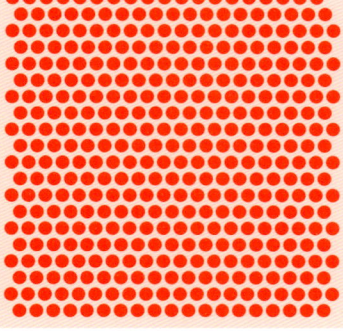

England 389 People per km^2

12

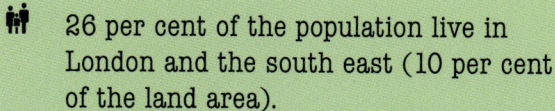

- 26 per cent of the population live in London and the south east (10 per cent of the land area).

- In London an average of 5,100 people live in a square kilometre.

- In the Highlands of Scotland an average of 8 people live in a square kilometre.

- **Urban areas** make up only 9 percent of the land area of Britain, but 80 per cent of the population live there.

FACTS

North–South divide?

In England there is much talk of a North-South divide, contrasting the poorer industrial north with the richer, less industrialised south. But where is the boundary between the two areas? Some researchers recently suggested a dividing line based on how long people lived and on the price of houses. It divides the Midlands in two – Nottingham is in the North, Leicester in the South; Birmingham is in the North and Warwick in the South!

North-South divide line?

England
50,800,000

Nottingham -
- Leicester
Birmingham -
- Warwick

Wales
3,000,000

The map (above) and diagram (left) show the population of the different parts of Britain. England is much more densely populated that the rest of the country.

Town and Country

Eight out of ten people live in towns and cities. It is very different living in a large urban area and in a village – or even on an isolated Scottish island.

The urban areas

In 2001, around 42 per cent of the population lived in the top 25 urban areas in Britain. An urban area includes the built-up area around the main cities on the map. This gives a better picture of where people live than population within the city's administrative boundaries, which is normally a lot smaller than the built-up area around that city.

Urban and rural contrasts

London is the most densely populated part of Britain and one of the most densely populated places in Europe (only central Paris and Brussels are denser). The top 10 most densely populated council areas are all in London.

people per
square kilometre
6 000
3 000
0

Edinburgh
452,000

Glasgow
1,168,000

Newcastle and Gateshead
880,000

Belfast
483,000

Middlesbrough
365,000

Manchester
2,240,000

Liverpool
816,000

Leeds and Bradford
1,500,000

Hull
301,000

Birkenhead
320,000

Sheffield
641,000

Stoke on Trent
362000

Nottingham
666,000

Leicester
441,000

Birmingham
2,284,000

Bristol
551,000

Coventry
336,000

London
8,278,000

Swansea
271,000

Reading and Wokingham
370,000

Cardiff
328,000

Southampton
304,000

Bournemouth
384,000

Brighton and Worthing
461,000

Portsmouth
442,000

At the top is Kensington and Chelsea, with 15,174 people per square kilometre. Of the 10 least densely populated areas, 8 are in Scotland, 1 in northern England and 1 in Wales. There are 8 people per square kilometre in Scotland's Highland area and 9 in the Outer Hebrides. The population of the Outer Hebrides is declining faster than anywhere else in Britain.

When is a city a city?

The words 'city' and 'town' are both used to describe big urban settlements. For a town to call itself a city, it has to be given approval by Parliament and the monarch. Some towns are called cities because they are the site of an old **cathedral**, such as Ely (top right) in Cambridgeshire. In Britain there are now 66 cities. Not all major urban areas are cities. Reading and Birkenhead, for example, are not cities. By contrast, the city of St Davids in Wales has a population of only 1,800 and the city of Wells, a population of 10,400. Both are cities because each has a cathedral.

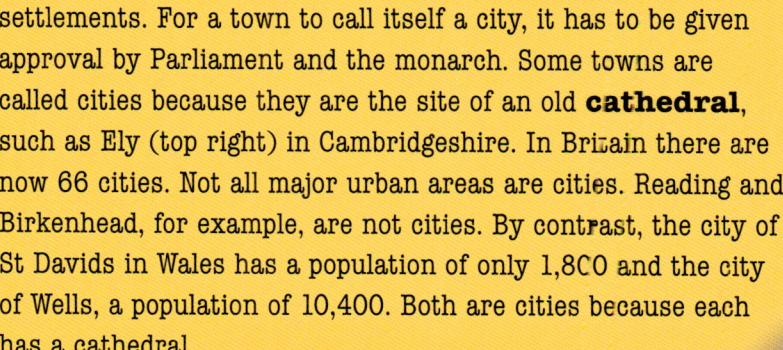

Shetland
Islands

FOULA

Isolated living

Foula is Britain's most remote **inhabited** island. The island is about 6 kilometres long and 4 kilometres wide, a mixture of cliffs, **peat bogs**, marshes and some grazing land. There are no trees. It is around 32 kilometres from the mainland of Shetland, and is only slightly closer to London than to Reykjavik, the capital of Iceland. In 1881, 267 people lived there, but now there are around 25 people. In winter, the ferry often does not run for weeks and food has to be flown in on a small plane that comes when the wind is not too strong. The telephone arrived in the 1960s, running water and electricity in the 1980s and broadband more recently. As one islander has said: 'Everyone has to have a roof over their heads and ours is here, that's all. We're just getting on with our lives.'

Orkney
Islands

SCOTLAND

How We Live

The homes we live in and the number of people we share our home with have a major influence on our health and well being. There have been many changes in recent years.

The number of homes

Since 1971, the number of homes has grown by 30 per cent while the population has only grown by 8 per cent. The largest increase has come in people who live by themselves, rising from 3 million in 1971 to 7 million in 2005. At the same time the number of homes where children live has declined.

Married or not?

In 1981, married couples made up 64 per cent of all homes. In 1991 this fell to 55 per cent and by 2001 it reached 45 per cent. In some areas, such as parts of Dorset, married couples make up almost 60 per cent of all homes, but in inner London they make up less than 25 per cent of all homes.

Marriage is on the decline, with more couples deciding to live together without marrying. While the number of marriages has decreased, the age at which people first marry has increased over the last 35 years, for men from 25 to 32 and for women from 23 to 30.

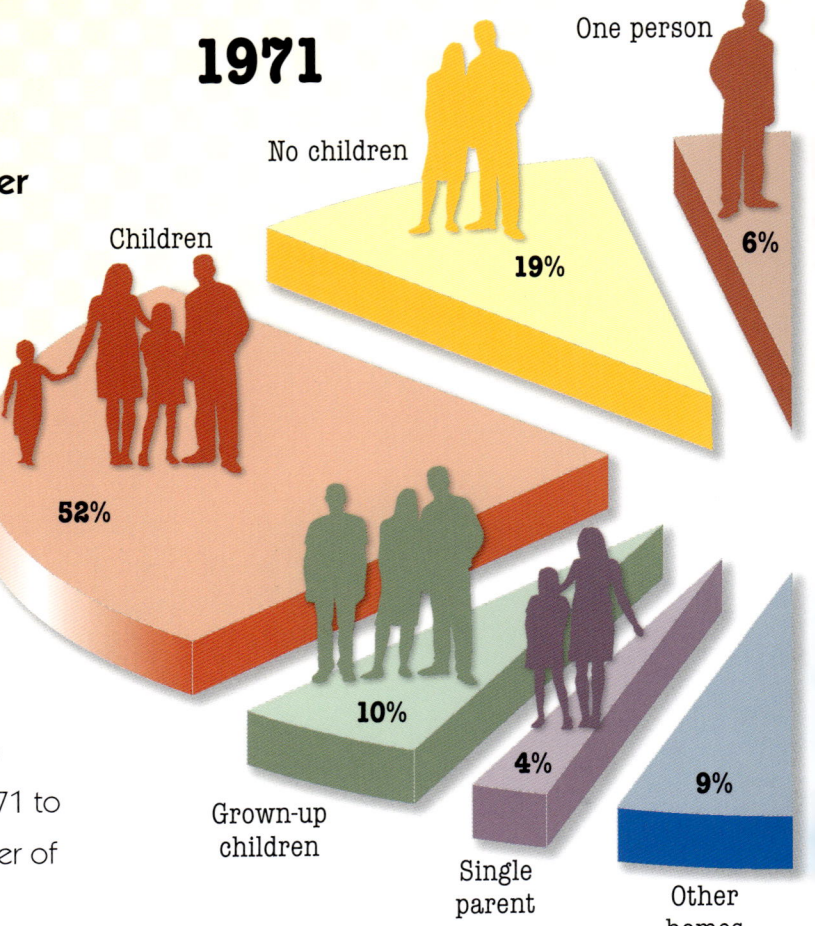

1971

Children 52%

No children 19%

One person 6%

Grown-up children 10%

Single parent 4%

Other homes 9%

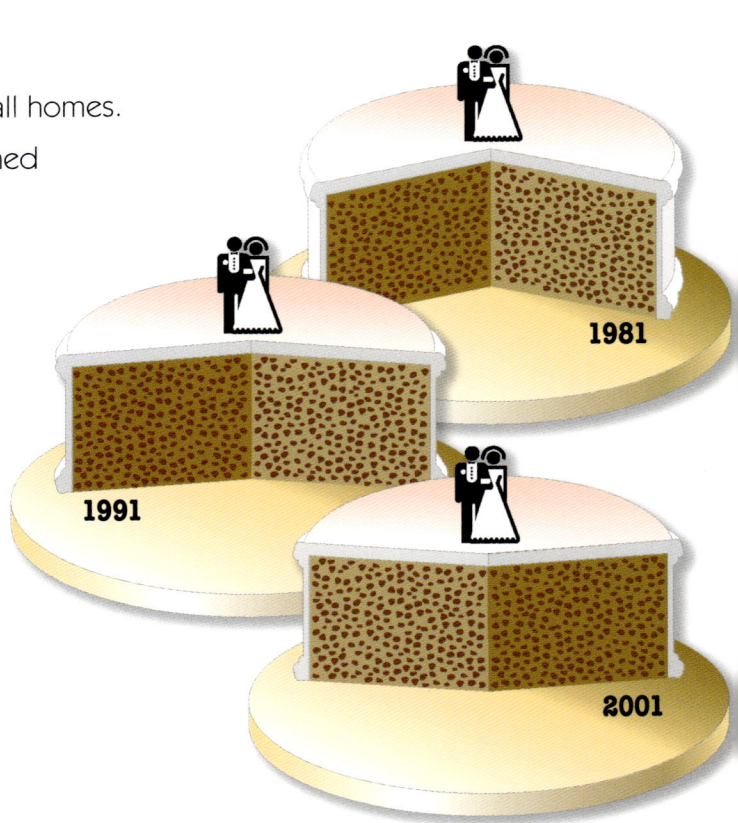

1981

1991

2001

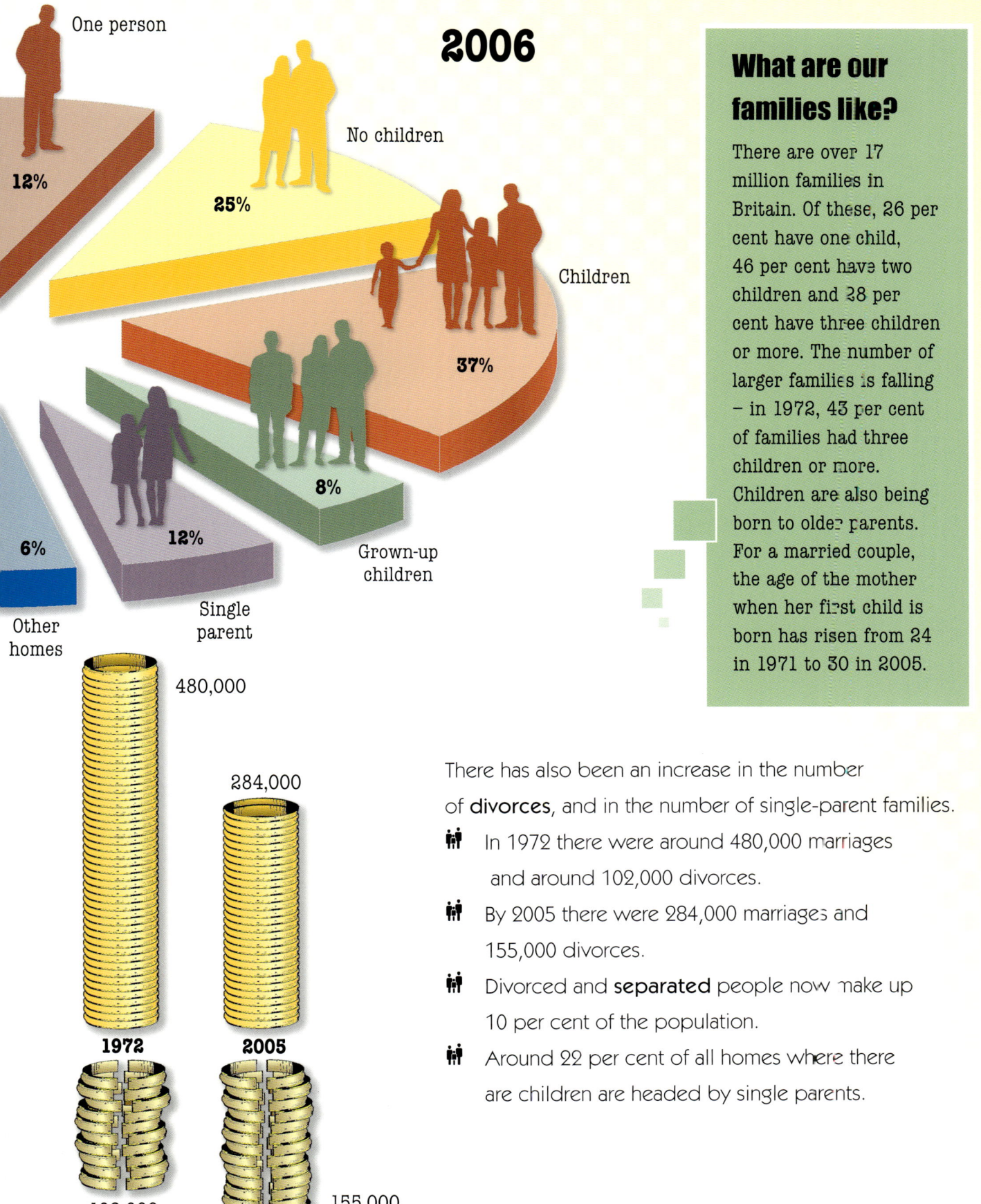

2006

One person

12%

No children

25%

Children

37%

Grown-up children

8%

Single parent

12%

Other homes

6%

480,000

284,000

1972

2005

102,000

155,000

There has also been an increase in the number of **divorces**, and in the number of single-parent families.

- In 1972 there were around 480,000 marriages and around 102,000 divorces.
- By 2005 there were 284,000 marriages and 155,000 divorces.
- Divorced and **separated** people now make up 10 per cent of the population.
- Around 22 per cent of all homes where there are children are headed by single parents.

Multicultural Britain

Britain today contains people from many different countries. In recent years the most significant reason for our increasing population has been the number of people coming to live in Britain from countries all over the world.

Our multicultural population

In 2001, 92 per cent of the population of Britain was described as white while 8 per cent had different **racial** origins. These people are sometimes described as coming from **ethnic minorities**. The chart below shows the main different groupings.

A multicultural crowd wait to greet the Queen. The Union Jack is Britain's flag and is a symbol of unity.

The racial origin of the 8 per cent of Britain's non-white population

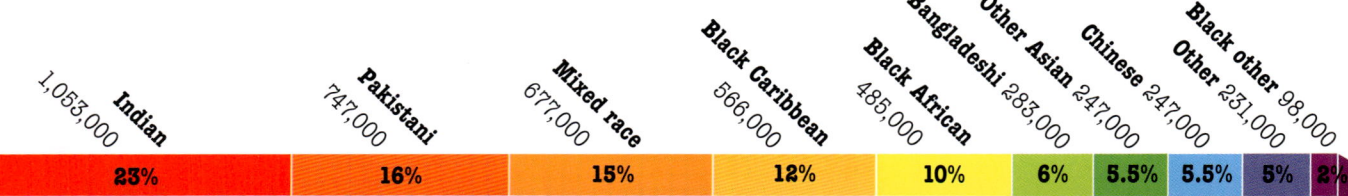

Indian 1,053,000	Pakistani 747,000	Mixed race 677,000	Black Caribbean 566,000	Black African 485,000	Bangladeshi 283,000	Other Asian 247,000	Chinese 247,000	Black other 98,000 / Other 231,000
23%	16%	15%	12%	10%	6%	5.5%	5.5%	5% 2%

Religion

One aspect of the increasing diversity of people in Britain is the mixture of **religions** that are adhered to. In 2001 around three-quarters of Britain's population claimed a religious identity. Over 70 per cent (around 31 million) were Christian. For other religions the figures were:

Muslim	Hindu	Sikh	Jewish	Buddhist
1,590,000	559,000	336,000	267,000	152,000

- Overall there are around 4.6 million people from ethnic minorities in Britain.
- This figure has grown from around 3 million in 1991.
- Minority populations are growing faster than white populations – with the fastest growth coming in the Chinese community.

The population mix varies greatly in different parts of Britain. In 2001:

- 1 per cent of Northern Ireland's population was from an ethnic minority,
- 2 per cent in Wales and Scotland,
- 9 per cent in England (and it is estimated that this has now risen to over 11 per cent).
- London is the most diverse part of Britain
- Around 78 per cent of all Black Africans and 62 per cent of all Black **Caribbeans** live in London; only 19 per cent of Pakistanis live there.
- Newham, in London, had the most diverse population with only 39.5 per cent of its population being white.

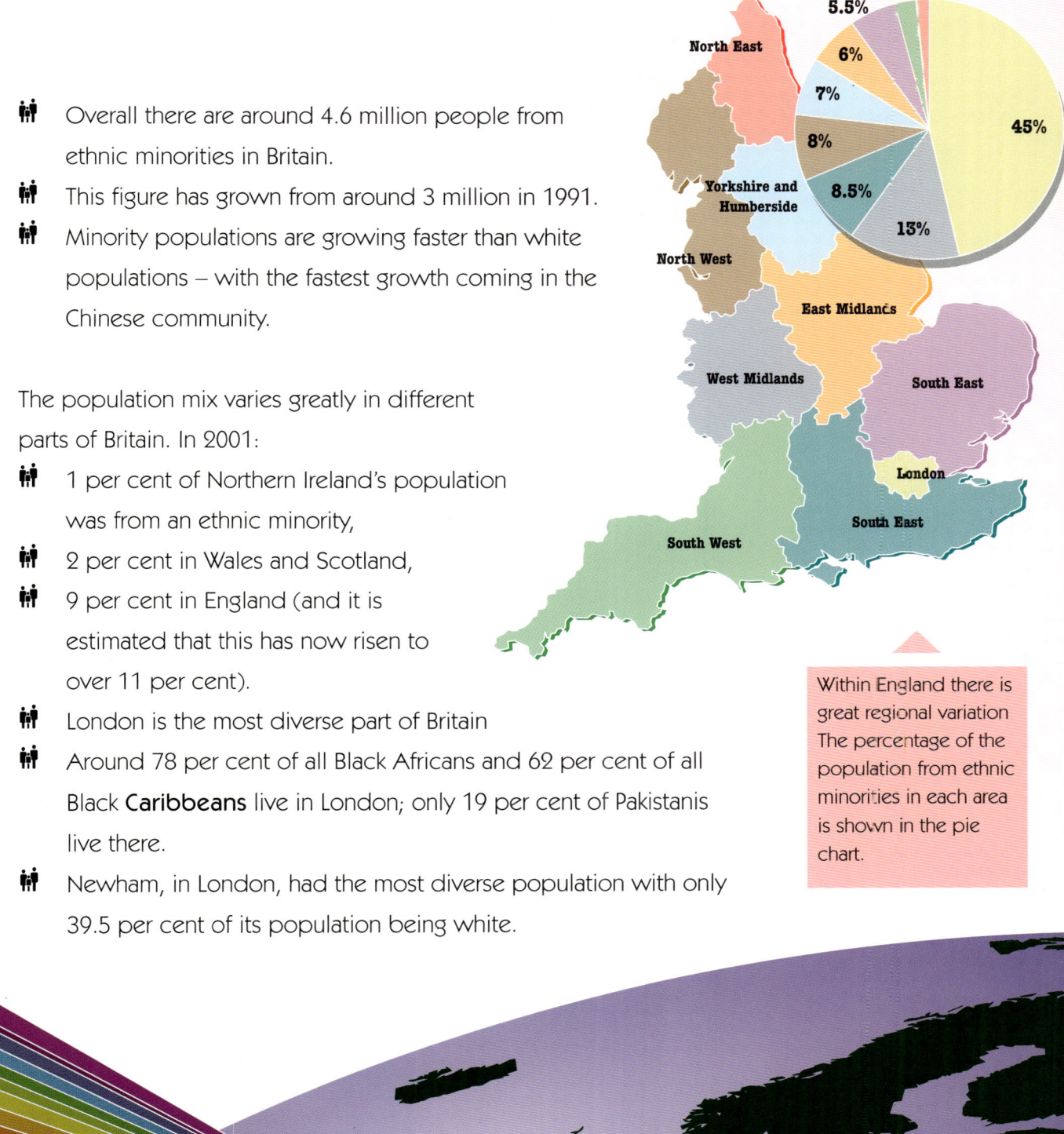

Within England there is great regional variation The percentage of the population from ethnic minorities in each area is shown in the pie chart.

What Does it Mean to be British?

In addition to the multicultural communities of Britain, the white population of Britain is also diverse. There are many regional differences within Britain.

A British citizen

If you are a **British citizen**, then you are able to obtain a British **passport** and travel in and out of Britain freely. Anyone born in Britain before 1983 is a British citizen. After 1983 it was also necessary for one parent to be a British citizen or to be legally settled in Britain. It is possible to apply to become a British citizen. This requires you to show that you have been **legally resident** for at least five years (three if married to a British citizen) and to show that you have a knowledge of English and of life in Britain. There is a test to pass.

If you are accepted, there is a **citizenship ceremony** at which you are formally accepted as a British citizen.

You will need to take the following pledge:

I will give my loyalty to the United Kingdom and respect its rights and freedoms. I will uphold its democratic values. I will observe its laws faithfully and fulfil my duties and obligations as a British citizen.

Regional variety

The way we speak can identify where we come from. A Geordie (from Newcastle), a Cockney (from London) and a Scouser (from Liverpool) all have distinctive accents. Some people even speak a different language, such as Gaelic, spoken in the Outer Hebrides, and Welsh, spoken in North Wales. Even in English, there can be many ways of saying the same thing. The map below shows the wide variety of ways in which 'left-handed' is said in different parts of the country. Instead of 'handed', the term 'fisted' or 'pawed' might be used in parts of England. In Scotland the words 'handit', 'fistit' or even 'klookit' are quite common.

How English is Cornwall?

When the Anglo-Saxons and Danes settled in England, they did not settle much of Cornwall. The **Celtic people** who lived there kept their old traditions. Some wish to revive these traditions, promoting the Cornish language (Kernewek) and greater independence for Cornwall (Kernow). There are language and musical links with other Celtic areas – particularly Brittany, Wales and Ireland. It is certainly less English than Sussex.

British passport

A passport is a very important document that allows you to travel to other countries and to return freely to Britain. To travel to some countries (such as other countries in the **European Union**) all you will need is your passport. For other countries you may also need to obtain a **visa** (official permission) from that country. A passport contains your photograph and other information to identify you. This information is stored on a **microchip** embedded in the passport.

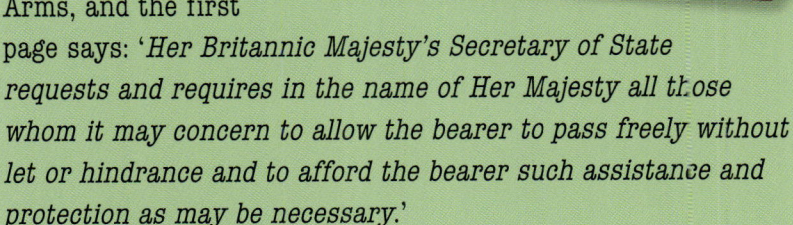

No passport for the Queen

The cover of a British passport features the Royal Arms, and the first page says: 'Her Britannic Majesty's Secretary of State requests and requires in the name of Her Majesty all those whom it may concern to allow the bearer to pass freely without let or hindrance and to afford the bearer such assistance and protection as may be necessary.'

As a British passport is issued in the name of Her Majesty, it is unnecessary for her to possess one.

Migration Before 1945

There have always been people coming to Britain and people leaving the country. Migration plays an important part in population change and in the great variety of people who live in Britain.

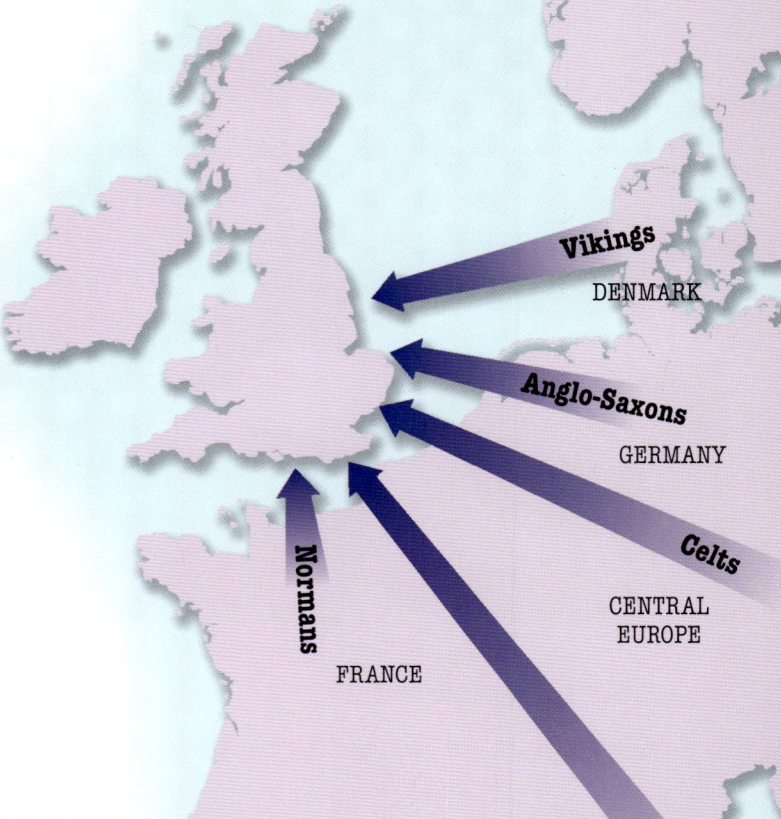

Vikings
DENMARK

Anglo-Saxons
GERMANY

Celts
CENTRAL EUROPE

Normans

FRANCE

Romans
ITALY

Early settlers

The original population grew from a number of different groups of people.

- Celtic people from central Europe settled here before the Romans.
- After the Romans, there were various invasions, first bringing the Anglo-Saxons from Germany in the fifth century. The name England (Angle-Land) comes from them.
- They were followed by the Vikings (from Denmark and Scandinavia).
- The French came after the Norman Conquest in 1066 (the Normans who had Viking origins, came from Normandy, in northern France).

Religious emigration

Many **puritans** (radical Christians) left Britain because they could not practice their faith freely. The 'Pilgrim Fathers' were one such group, originally from the East Midlands. In September 1620, they left Plymouth in Devon on board the *Mayflower*. After 66 days they reached Cape Cod, where they established the colony of New Plymouth, the second British colony in North America.

In Scotland, Wales, Ireland and Cornwall, the Celtic peoples survived, although the Vikings settled in coastal areas, and the Normans came after 1066.

For nearly 1,000 years these groups have mixed together. Some surnames reflect this original mix: Brown (Anglo-Saxon), Sinclair (French), Thorpe (Danish), Lloyd (Celtic).

Religious immigration

While some left Britain to escape **persecution**, others came to escape persecution in their own country. In 1685 Louis XIV, the King of France, expelled Protestant Christians. Known as Huguenots, around 50,000 came to settle in Britain. In London, many settled in Spitalfields, to the east of the City of London. As time went by, they moved away. Jewish migrants from Eastern Europe followed them to the same area. As they, too, moved away, Bangladeshis settled there. All of them have been involved in weaving and making clothing.

Emigration in the nineteenth century

Famine and poverty led to much emigration in the nineteenth century. In the 1840s the potato crop failed in Ireland, causing a famine. As a result over a million people emigrated to the USA and Canada. Many Scots also emigrated to escape poverty. It has been estimated that between 1870 and 1913 around 6 million more people left Britain than came here. Around 55 per cent went to the USA, and most of the others to Canada, Australia and New Zealand.

Escaping from Hitler

In the 1930s, the German dictator, Adolf Hitler began a violent persecution of the Jewish community. Many Jews from Europe came to settle in Britain. Amongst them were 10,000 children, sent by their parents who were unable to escape. The photograph below shows children arriving at Southampton in 1939 to start a new life with new families. To give people shelter from persecution is to give them **asylum**.

Migration Since 1945

After the Second World War, the pattern of migration began to change. People from Britain continued to emigrate, but more people from different countries came to Britain. In 2006 around 191,000 more people came to Britain than left Britain: 400,000 people left and 591,000 arrived.

Emigration

With over 200,000 British citizens leaving Britain every year, levels of emigration are at their highest since before 1914.

- Over 64 per cent of those emigrating went to five countries: Australia, New Zealand, France, Spain and the USA.
- It is now estimated that 1 in 12 of all British nationals live aboard.
- There are over 40 countries with a British population of more than 10,000.
- Many people are retiring to other countries – for example over 250,000 homes in France are British-owned.

Turkey 21,500

Serbia & Montenegro 33,500

The *Empire Windrush*

In 1948 the *Empire Windrush* docked at Kingston, Jamaica, to collect some Jamaicans who were returning to Britain to work in the Royal Air Force. There was extra space on board, and 492 Jamaicans paid £28 for the trip to Britain. The arrival of the *Empire Windrush* at Tilbury Docks, near London, on 22 June 1948 became the symbol of the start of immigration from the West Indies.

Expanded European Union

In 2004, 10 countries, mainly in Eastern Europe, were admitted into the **European Union**. Their citizens were able to come to Britain easily. Many have come and have found employment in the agricultural, building and hospitality industries, where there are labour shortages. The largest number have settled in East Anglia. By December 2007, over 500,000 Poles had registered to work in Britain, along with around 250,000 from Slovakia, Lithuania, the Czech Republic, Latvia, Hungary and Estonia.

Where asylum seekers come from

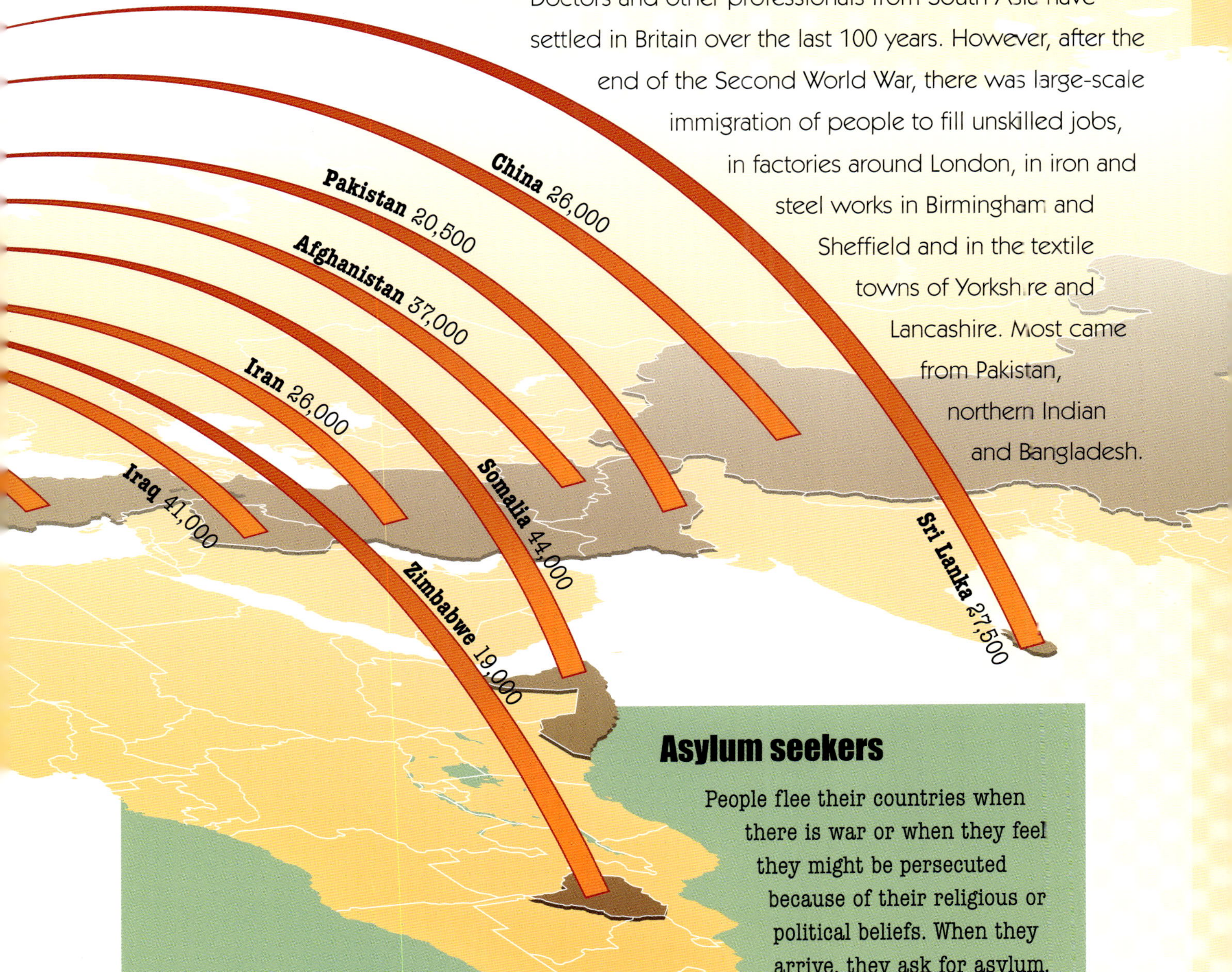

Immigration from South Asia

Doctors and other professionals from South Asia have settled in Britain over the last 100 years. However, after the end of the Second World War, there was large-scale immigration of people to fill unskilled jobs, in factories around London, in iron and steel works in Birmingham and Sheffield and in the textile towns of Yorkshire and Lancashire. Most came from Pakistan, northern Indian and Bangladesh.

China 26,000

Pakistan 20,500

Afghanistan 37,000

Iran 26,000

Iraq 41,000

Somalia 44,000

Zimbabwe 19,000

Sri Lanka 27,500

Asylum seekers

People flee their countries when there is war or when they feel they might be persecuted because of their religious or political beliefs. When they arrive, they ask for asylum. The government has to decide whether the asylum seeker is escaping persecution or should be returned to their own country. In 2006, 21 per cent of asylum seekers were allowed to stay. The number of asylum applications rose from 32,500 in 1997 to 84,000 in 2002, and has since declined to 23,500 in 2007. The diagram shows where asylum seekers came from between 1997 and 2006.

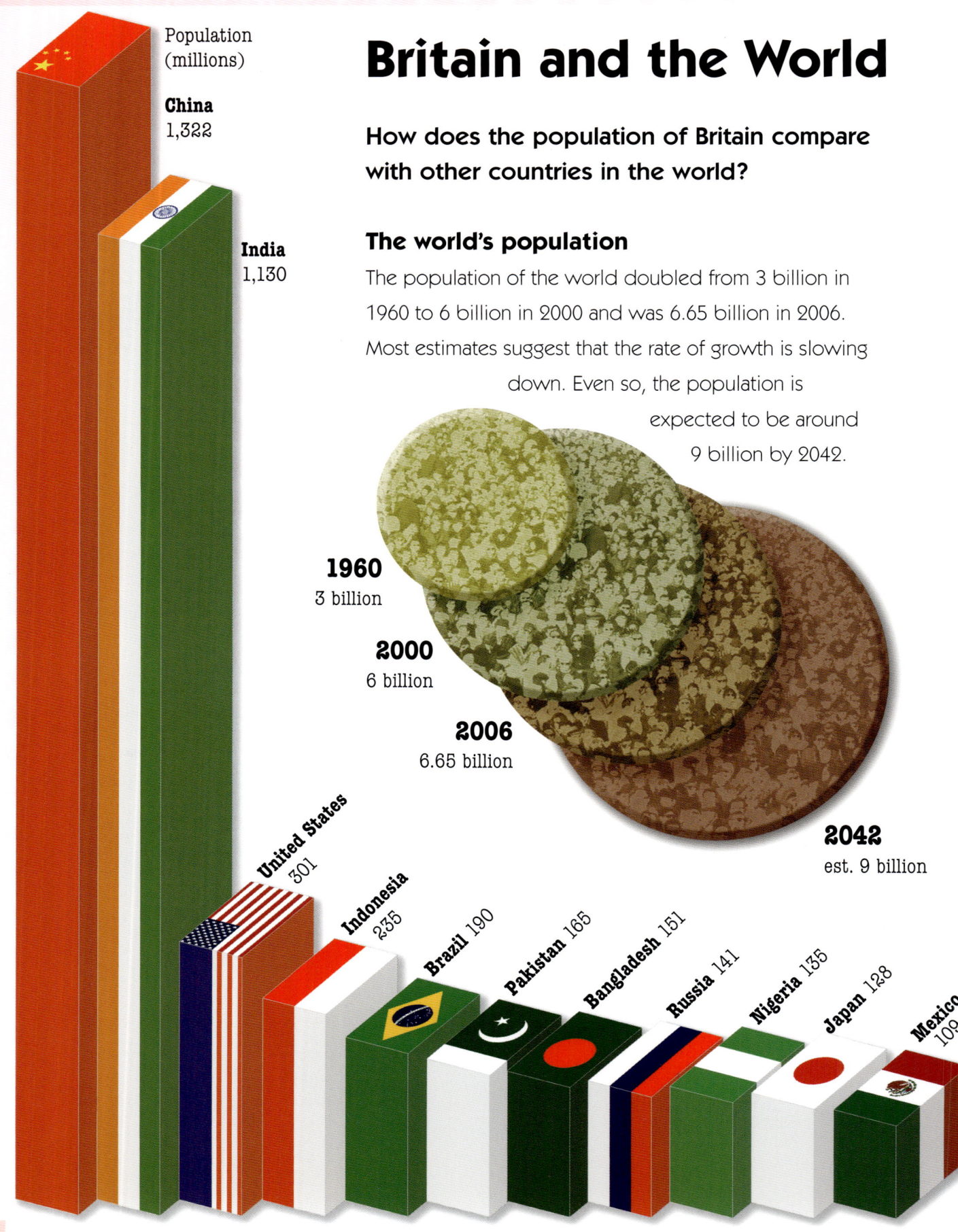

Population (millions)

China
1,322

India
1,130

Britain and the World

How does the population of Britain compare with other countries in the world?

The world's population

The population of the world doubled from 3 billion in 1960 to 6 billion in 2000 and was 6.65 billion in 2006. Most estimates suggest that the rate of growth is slowing down. Even so, the population is expected to be around 9 billion by 2042.

1960
3 billion

2000
6 billion

2006
6.65 billion

2042
est. 9 billion

United States 301

Indonesia 235

Brazil 190

Pakistan 165

Bangladesh 151

Russia 141

Nigeria 135

Japan 128

Mexico 109

Britain's population in 1960 was around 52 million. If our population had grown at the same rate as the world's, it would have been 104 million in 2000 and would be 156 million by 2042. Imagine how overcrowded and short of resources we would be. Then think about what is happening to the world.

The size of Britain

Britain has one of the largest populations in Europe but it was 22nd in the world in 2006. Look at the chart below. There are probably some surprises.

Britain is the third largest country in the European Union. Wales has a population similar to Latvia or Lithuania, Scotland to Finland or Slovakia and Northern Ireland to Estonia or Slovenia.

FACTS

- Britain is the 47th most densely populated country in the world at 251 people per square kilometre, just behind Jamaica and Vietnam and ahead of Germany and Pakistan. The densest small countries are Monaco and Macau (both 16,300 people per square kilometre). The densest large country is Bangladesh with 1,044 people per square kilometre. Australia has under 3 and Mongolia under 2 people per square kilometre.

- Britain's birth rate (births per 1,000 people) is 11. Niger has the highest rate at 50. Hong Kong has the lowest at 7.

- Average life expectancy in Britain is 78.7 years. In Japan it is 82 (with Andorra at 83.5 being the highest), while in Swaziland it is 32.

- Electricity consumption:12th behind Brazil and South Korea, ahead of Italy and Spain.

  Oil consumption: 13th behind Saudi Arabia and France, ahead of Italy and Iran.

  Mobile phones: 9th behind Germany and Italy, ahead of Indonesia and Pakistan.

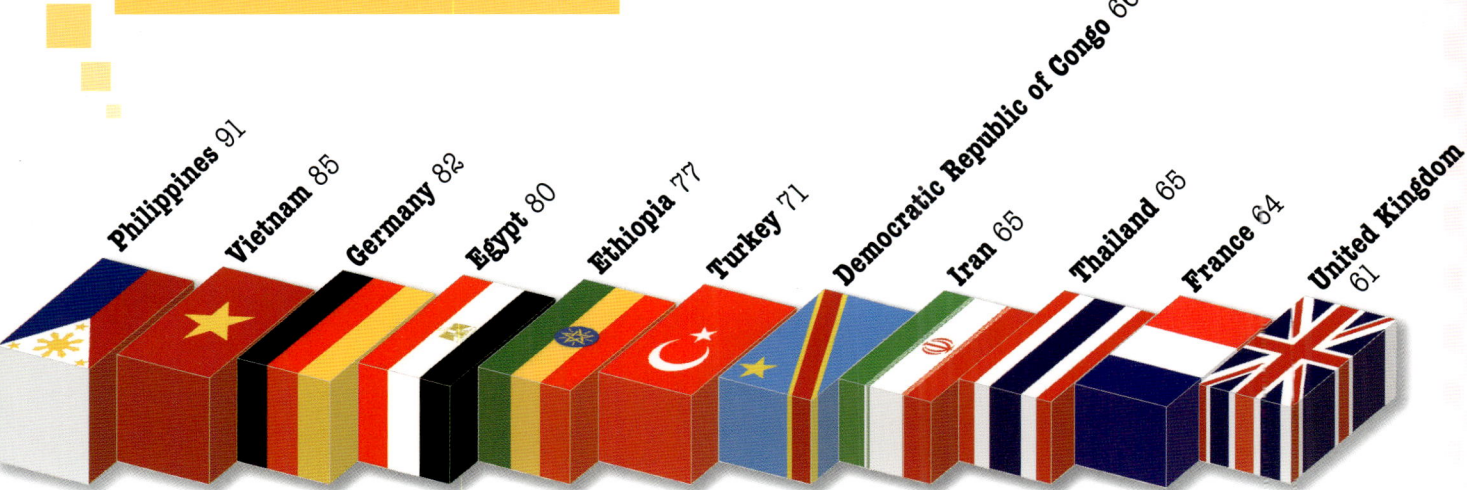

Philippines 91 · Vietnam 85 · Germany 82 · Egypt 80 · Ethiopia 77 · Turkey 71 · Democratic Republic of Congo 66 · Iran 65 · Thailand 65 · France 64 · United Kingdom 61

Discussion Points

Here are a few suggestions for discussion points on the population of Britain (the page numbers indicate where the topic is covered in the book).

- Why do you think it is important to know how many people live in Britain? (**pages 4–5**)

- If you were planning a census, what questions would you ask? To see the actual form used for England in the 2001 census, visit **www.statistics.gov.uk/census2001/pdfs/H1.pdf** (**pages 4–5**)

- Look at the diagram showing the growth of the population of England (**page 6**). Why did the population fall between 1300 and 1400 and why did it rise after 1400?

- What factors can cause the population to change? (**pages 8–9**)

- Look at the population pyramids and the Facts box on **pages 10** and **11**. What is happening to Britain's population?

- Why do you think England is more densely populated than the rest of Britain? (**pages 12–13**)

- What would you like and what would you dislike about living on Foula? (**page 15**)

- What reasons can you think of for the shrinking size of the British family? (**page 17**)

- Why do you think London is more multicultural than the rest of Britain? (**pages 18–19**)

- Give some reasons for why some people leave Britain and others come here to live. (**pages 22–25**)

- Under what circumstances would you give asylum to those who were seeking it here? (**pages 24–25**)

- Look at the chart of the most populated countries in the world on **pages 26–27**. Are you surprised by some of the countries that appear? Find out more about them.

Websites

The Office for National Statistics collects information on the population of the UK. The page below lists lots of topics and more will be shown if you click on the 'Focus on' heading.

www.statistics.gov.uk/glance

There is also a lot of information from the censuses available. For England and Wales, visit: **www.statistics.gov.uk/census** For Scotland, visit the General Register Office for Scotland: **www.gro-scotland.gov.uk/census** For Northern Ireland visit the Northern Ireland Statistics and Research Agency (NISRA): **www.nisra.gov.uk**

For an interactive chart of UK population change, visit: **http://news.bbc.co.uk/1/hi/uk/4045261.stm**

As an example of immigration into Britain, there is much information on the *Empire Windrush* (see page 24), including the stories of a number of people who arrived on the boat: **www.bbc.co.uk/history/british/modern/arrival_01.shtml**

For the latest on the population of countries of the world and their uses of resources visit the CIA *World Factbook*: **www.cia.gov/library/publications/the-world-factbook**

Note to parents and teachers: Every effort has been made by the Publishers to ensure that these websites are suitable for children, that they are of the highest educational value, and that they contain no inappropriate or offensive material. However, because of the nature of the Internet, it is impossible to guarantee that the contents of these sites will not be altered. We strongly advise that Internet access is supervised by a responsible adult.

Immigration Time Line

1838 Complete abolition of slavery throughout British Empire.

1881 Jews flee Russia to escape attack. By 1914, 130,000 settled in London.

1905 Alien Act passed, the first time immigration to Britain restricted.

1920 Indian doctors begin to arrive in Britain.

1931 League of Coloured People formed to fight discrimination.

1939 By this year over 60,000 Jews reached Britain escaping from persecution in Europe. Also 160,000 Poles arrive.

1948 The *Empire Windrush* brings nearly 500 immigrants from Jamaica, the start of immigration from the West Indies.

1955 Large-scale immigration from India begins.

1959 Claudia Jones first runs the Caribbean street carnival in London that became the Notting Hill Carnival.

1962 Commonwealth Immigration Act started to control immigration to the UK. It limits Commonwealth immigration to 45,000 a year.

1965 First Race Relations Act passed, banning discrimination in public places. Further Acts in 1968, 1976 and 2000 tackle discrimination in all areas of daily life.

1972 30,000 Asians expelled from Uganda by Idi Amin arrive in Britain.

1978 The first of 16,500 Vietnamese boat people arrive in Britain.

1981 Rioting in Brixton (in London) and Toxteth (in Liverpool) had racial causes. Immigration further tightened in new Immigration Act.

2002 Peak of 84,000 asylum applications.

2004 EU enlargement results in major immigration from Poland.

2008 Immigration Act links immigration to skills needed in Britain.

Glossary

agricultural Used to describe anything to do with farming.

asylum The right for a person to stay in one country when fleeing from persecution in another.

British citizen A person who officially belongs to Britain, either by being born here or because the Government has given that person citizenship based on the length of time lived here and the contribution made to the country.

Caribbean Describing a person who lives in or originally come from the West Indies. The Caribs were the original inhabitants of that area.

cathedral The main church of a particular area, called a diocese, that is looked after by a bishop.

Celtic people People who originally came from central Europe and are now the longest-establish settlers in western Scotland, Ireland, Wales and Cornwall, having reached these areas before the Roman conquest.

census An accurate counting of all the people who live in a country on a particular day.

citizenship ceremony A special ceremony at which people who have come to Britain to live are given British citizenship.

distribution The number of things at particular places, so the population distribution indicates the number of people living at specific places.

divorce When two people who are married decide to legally end their marriage and live separately.

emigration The movement of people away from a particular country.

ethnic minorities Groups of people in a country who originally came from different parts of the world and whose numbers are small when compared with the number of people who have always traditionally lived here.

European Union (EU) A group of European countries that work together. There is freedom for people in the European Union to move between the countries of the EU, which are: Austria, Belgium, Bulgaria, Cyprus, Czech Republic, Denmark, Estonia, Finland, France, Germany, Greece, Hungary, Ireland, Italy, Latvia, Lithuania, Luxembourg, Malta, Netherlands, Poland, Portugal, Romania, Slovakia, Slovenia, Spain, Sweden and the United Kingdom.

immigration The movement of people into one country from other countries. A person who comes to one country from another is called an immigrant.

industrialisation The process by which an agricultural country develops its own industries.

infant mortality A measure of the number of babies who die at birth or shortly afterwards.

infectious Describing an illness that can easily be passed from person to person.

inhabit To live in a particular place. Such a place is said to be inhabited.

legally resident Describing someone who is officially allowed to live in a country. An illegal immigrant is someone who is not officially allowed to live in the country.

microchip A very small electronic circuit made on a silicon chip. A microchip in a passport stores information about the passport holder.

migration The movement of people in and out of a country or a particular area within a country.

multicultural Describing a society where people from many parts of the world live together. London is one of the most multicultural cities in the world.

passport An official document that confirms the identity of the holder and allows a citizen of one country to travel easily to another.

peat bogs Infertile and poorly drained land made from peat, which is created from vegetation that has rotted over thousands of years.

persecution Treating a person in an unfair, illegal or cruel way.

population The number of people who live in a particular country or region. The population density is the number of people who live in a measured area, most usually a square kilometre.

population pyramid A diagram that shows how a particular population is divided between the sexes and between different age bands. A country undergoing industrialisation usually has a distribution shaped like a pyramid, hence the name.

predict Using current information to estimate what something may be in the future.

puritans The name given to radical Protestant Christians in the seventeenth century.

racial Describing people of a different race. The term 'race' can be used to describe people with different physical characteristics, such as different colours of skin.

religion a belief in a god or gods, and the activities, such as prayer and worship, that are linked to that belief.

separated Used to describe a married couple who are living apart but not divorced. This means that they remain legally married.

urban area Area of a country that is mostly covered with buildings. It can also describe the built-up area around a particular city. By contrast, a rural area is mainly covered in fields.

visa The permission given by one country for a citizen of another country to visit it. A British citizen needs a visa to visit China, for example.

Index